18422

Beethoven

THE GREAT COMPOSERS

BEETHOVEN

by

STANLEY SADIE

THOMAS Y. CROWELL COMPANY
New York

Contents

Illustrations

Illustrations

Grateful acknowledgements are made to the following for permission to reproduce copyright material: to *The Musical Times* for Plates III, IV (b), V, VII, Figures 1, 2, 5 and the illustration on the back cover; to the Beethoven House, Bonn, for Plates VI and VIII; to Philips Records for Plate I (a) and Figures 2 and 4; and to Guy Gravett and Glyndebourne Festival Opera for Plate IV (a) (the final scene from *Fidelio*, 1963).

Music Examples

Music Examples

Beethoven

Beethoven

I

Boyhood in Bonn

Music is an art which develops steadily from generation to generation. When Beethoven was born, in 1770, there were two great composers living: Mozart and Haydn. At this time, many people thought of music as nothing more than an agreeable form of entertainment. These two men were helping to enrich its capacity as an expression of human feeling. Beethoven carried it still further, into a language in which he could convey, and make us feel, the deepest of emotions and the sublimest of ideas.

Not that Beethoven was a philosopher; he was a musician, and only a musician. But in his music one can somehow detect a parallel with the other great events and movements of his time—the time of the French Revolution and the Napoleonic Wars, the time of such great writers as Schiller and Goethe or such a visionary as William Blake.

Like Bach and Mozart, Beethoven himself came from a family of musicians. The family was of Flemish origin. His grandfather had spent a working life typical of an eighteenth-century musician; he had come to Bonn in 1733 and had taken a job as court musician there, and being a man of unusual ability he had eventually become Kapellmeister (head of the musical establishment). Bonn, a town on the Rhine in western Germany, was like many other medium-sized or large German towns in that it was ruled by its own local prince, or 'Elector'. The Elector maintained his own court, with its own chapel, and its own small orchestra to provide musical entertainment. Beethoven's grandfather, Louis van Beethoven, was probably a very able Kapellmeister, although he spent much of his time away from music running a wine business.

His son Johann, Beethoven's father, was less distinguished. He was a singer in the chapel and a competent teacher of music, but of unstable character and in the later part of his life over-fond of drink. He was married, to the young widow of a former court valet, in 1767. In December 1770 their second child (their first died in infancy) was born, and was baptized Ludwig.

So the young Beethoven was brought up in an atmosphere where music was taken for granted. But when he was only three his grandfather died. As soon as his fingers were big enough, his father set him to work at learning the harpsichord (for pianos were then still a novelty, and a luxury) and the violin. Some ten years before, a sensation had been created by a child prodigy, by name Wolfgang Amadeus Mozart, whose father had taken him round Europe displaying his fantastic gifts to wondering audiences. Beethoven's father wanted to do the same with Ludwig, and made him practise hard every day; when he did show off the boy in public, he subtracted a couple of years from his age so as to make his gifts seem the greater.

Altogether, Beethoven didn't have a happy childhood. A friend of the family said that he and his two younger brothers 'were not brought up with kindness . . . their father was often very severe with them.' Another said he was 'shy and quiet, watching and thinking more than talking.' His father was often drunk; his mother seems to have been kindly and gentle, but a serious person who never smiled or laughed.

When he was about eight, Beethoven started lessons under other teachers than his father. The best and most important of these was C. G. Neefe, the court organist and himself a composer, under whom he studied from about 1779 to 1782. Neefe taught him to play Bach's forty-eight Preludes and Fugues (which were little known at this time and were the ideal instruction for him) and he supervised the boy's first attempts at composition. In 1782 Neefe was away from Bonn for a short time, leaving the eleven-year-old Ludwig (who had now left school to concentrate on music) to act as his deputy, and the next year Ludwig was given the responsibility of directing rehearsals of the theatre orchestra. He was barely thirteen when he was appointed assistant court organist—and it was just as well that he was earning some money, for the family finances were none too secure.

By this time Beethoven already had several promising compositions to his credit. They were mainly songs or piano music: rondos, three sonatas which he dedicated to the Elector, and various other short pieces. By the time he was fifteen he had also completed a set of three piano quartets (for piano, violin, viola and cello). They are not great music. But these pieces already show the beginnings of a strong musical personality. A few years later Beethoven used a movement from one of the quartets in a piano sonata:

The house where Beethoven was born

The entry for Beethoven's baptism in the
Register of St. Remigius's Church, Bonn:
17th December 1770

Ansicht vom Graben gegen den Kohlmarkt.

Rue du Graben vers le Kohlmarkt.

Vienna in the eighteenth century

Ex. 1. Piano sonata, Op. 2 No. 1

Slow

Besides his odd hours devoted to composition, Beethoven had to spend time at his duties in the court chapel and in his studies under Neefe. But Bonn, although a reasonably lively place artistically, was far away from the real artistic centres of Europe. So in 1787 Beethoven went—possibly at the Elector's suggestion, and expense—to Vienna. There he played before Mozart and others. But he had been there only two weeks when news came that his mother was seriously ill. He hastened back to Bonn, to find her dying of consumption. Her death depressed him greatly. Later in his life he wrote of her: 'She was to me such a good, loving mother, and indeed my best friend.'

So after a dark and miserable childhood Beethoven moved on to adolescence in a sad, disorganized home, without a mother's influence. The home had never been very well managed; one of Beethoven's schoolboy friends said, years later, that Beethoven had always been untidy and careless in his appearance. But now things were worse than ever. Beethoven's father was in a wretched state and it fell to Beethoven himself, at seventeen, to look after the family—his brothers of thirteen and eleven and a baby sister who very soon died. Two years later Johann van Beethoven was in such a condition that he could no longer perform his duties; he was sent away and part of his salary was paid to Beethoven.

This naturally made life easier for Beethoven and his brothers, and the next years seem to have been happier ones. Many friends, perhaps recognizing him as a growing genius, helped him, partly by giving him work as a teacher and partly just by their friendship. There was the van Breuning family, where the three sons and a daughter became affectionate and understanding friends, and remained close to him throughout his stormy life. There was his violin teacher, Franz Anton Ries. And there was the young Count Waldstein, who helped him in various ways, a piano being one of his most useful gifts; this was a friendship across the barriers of social class— barriers which Beethoven himself hardly recognized, for to him one man was much like another, whether rich or poor, noble or humble.

Beethoven was fortunate to have as his employer an Elector who had good musical taste and liked to spend much of his time listening to music. In 1788 the Elector decided to have operas given in his theatre. Beethoven, still a court organist, entered the opera orchestra as a viola player. Here he got to know the best operatic music of his time (including works by Mozart and Gluck) and he also got to know a great deal about the orchestra and instruments, knowledge which was to be very important to him in years to come. The orchestra he played in was a particularly good one. Probably it was for the wind players in it that he wrote an Octet and a Rondino. Wind music at this time was often used simply as a background to other activities; the Elector may well have heard strains like these, from the oboes, clarinets, bassoons and horns, as he sat eating his supper, or as he strolled through the gardens of his palace on a warm summer evening:

Ex. 2. Rondino for wind instruments

But the old way of life was changing. By 1794 Bonn had been invaded by the French armies; the Elector fled, and he never returned. Beethoven was to write no more music simply for the pleasure of a few noblemen. He knew his powers, and he knew he had the whole musical world to conquer.

In 1792, in fact, the twenty-two-year-old Beethoven had left Bonn for the last time. We don't know exactly why he left, but it is possible to guess. In 1790, Joseph Haydn had travelled through Bonn on the first of his journeys to London, and in 1792 he returned by the same route. At this time Haydn was recognized as the greatest living composer, and the musicians at Bonn naturally gave a special performance in his honour. Afterwards he met many of them. Not surprisingly, he was particularly impressed by Beethoven, and all the more so when the young genius showed him a cantata he had written. Quite possibly, Haydn invited Beethoven to Vienna, or at least persuaded the authorities at Bonn to give him leave for a period of study there.

But whatever the reason, the fact is that Beethoven left Bonn towards the end of the year, and never returned. He bade an affectionate farewell to his many childhood friends, and, although war was raging in the country he had to pass through, he set out on his journey. Beethoven, armed with a bundle of manuscripts, his unique musical genius and his immense determination, arrived in Vienna, the city where Mozart had just died and where Haydn was living. In this great centre of the musical world he settled, to make his career there.

Figure 1. The Bonn Market-Place: an eighteenth-century drawing

II

The Young Virtuoso

With his arrival in Vienna, Beethoven moved into a completely different musical atmosphere. In Bonn, musical activities centred on a single court, its chapel and its theatre; in Vienna too there was a court, but also many churches and theatres attended by the city's large population, and in addition innumerable private homes where regular music-making was the rule.

Beethoven was now faced by two tasks: to deepen his knowledge of composition, and to earn his livelihood. At first, he did not have to worry too much about his livelihood, for he still received a salary as a Bonn court musician. But soon he had to think about this problem—which only the year before had finally defeated Mozart.

Clearly he was too young and too little-known to expect a court appointment, and anyway he probably didn't want to spend his life as servant of a court. So he had to spend much of his time teaching. Letters of introduction which he brought from Bonn helped him to find pupils. The same letters also gave him entry into the drawing-rooms of musical patrons. Here he made a great impression. There had been, and still were, many other fine pianists, but Beethoven had a force and vitality in his playing which were unequalled. In those days a pianist was expected not simply to play a few pieces but also to improvise—to make up a new piece as he went along. Beethoven was a master of this art. His improvisations had not merely the usual brilliance and decoration expected from a virtuoso, but also vivid fantasy and great emotional power.

There was another reason, too, why Beethoven soon became a noted figure in Vienna's musical life. If he entered a fashionable drawing-room, he expected to be treated as an equal, not as an inferior. He felt that his artistic gifts put him on a level with the noblest of his patrons. When he played, he expected to be given full attention. The musical people of Vienna were fascinated by this curious man, and they could recognize that he was an artist very much out of the ordinary who really deserved the attention he demanded.

Beethoven also began to build up a reputation by playing at concerts. In those days concerts were organized rather differently from today. There were a few regular series of concerts open to the public, and piano recitals were practically unknown. Sometimes a well-known musician would organize a concert himself; Beethoven several times helped his friends by playing in their concerts, or he played at concerts in aid of charity. But it was a long time before he tried organizing one for himself. Outside Vienna conditions were rather different. Beethoven occasionally went on concert tours, arranging concerts in such cities as Prague or Dresden and playing in some of the smaller towns as well.

He was busy in these years, too, studying the technique of composition. Even for someone of great natural ability, like Mozart or Schubert, composition demanded long and concentrated technical study, which no amount of inspiration could short-circuit—and in any case Beethoven did not have natural gifts of this kind but always found composing hard and strenuous work. He started his studies under Joseph Haydn. But they did not go very well. Haydn, an old man in his sixties with a lifetime of composing behind him, was set in his ways, and he must have found the impatient young Beethoven's forceful ideas eccentric and lacking in taste. And Beethoven perhaps felt that Haydn's criticisms were unsympathetic and discouraging whenever he produced really original work. Later, Beethoven complained that Haydn's teaching had been too easy-going for him.

At the beginning of 1794 Haydn departed on a trip to London, and it was probably just before then that Beethoven found a new master in Albrechtsberger, a much lesser composer than Haydn, but an experienced teacher, particularly in the difficult field of counterpoint. About the same time he had lessons with another theorist, Schenk, and also with an eminent composer, Antonio Salieri—an Italian with much experience in opera, who could be particularly helpful in teaching him how to handle the human voice and to set words in suitable style. The fact that Beethoven had as many as four teachers (and there may have been still more) shows clearly how determined he was to achieve the proper mastery of his art, and how keen he was to learn as much as he could in the shortest possible time.

Beethoven learned much from other men; but his music bore the marks of his own character. This is especially true of his piano music; when writing for his own instrument he was able to give freer rein to his imagination and feelings. Among the earliest of his compositions which are still played today

Figure 2. The young Beethoven

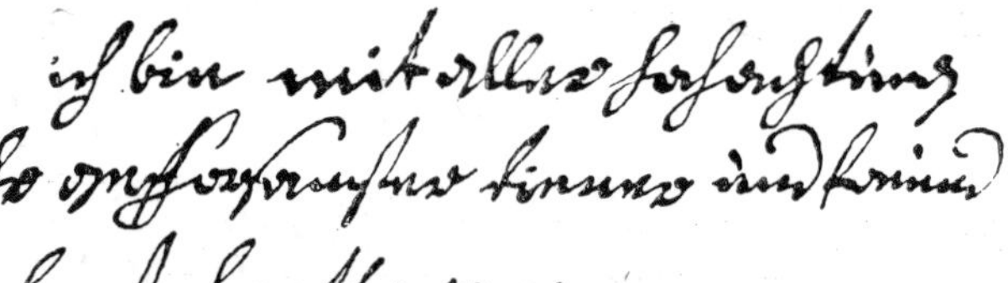

Figure 3. Beethoven's handwriting, from a letter of 1787

are the three piano sonatas, Op. 2, which he dedicated to Haydn. In these we can see how this strong-willed, defiant young man's personality comes out in his music. This is the start of the first sonata:

23

Ex. 3. Piano sonata, Op. 2 No. 1

Fast

Just like the young composer himself, this music is full of dynamic energy, with its rising phrases and its marked accents. It is this note of urgency and excitement that is so typical of Beethoven's works in these early years; and it forced the musical public of Vienna into taking notice of him.

Looking at that theme again, one could very well say that it isn't really a particularly good tune. It certainly has none of the beauty, or singing quality, that one usually finds at the beginning of a sonata by Mozart or Haydn. But this only helps to show how Beethoven, although using the same forms, harmonies and general styles as Mozart and Haydn, was opening up a new musical world. His sonata is not less good because its melodies are less interesting in themselves, for Beethoven was using all kinds of other ways of creating musical interest. Especially important, in this brief theme (and in many others), is his use of dynamics—the interest here largely depends on the music's getting louder and the accents being sharply made, as well as the mounting excitement as the phrases get shorter. In the last movement of the same sonata there is again much vigorous excitement which comes from the sharp contrasts of loud and soft, and from the rushing triplets which go on for most of the movement.

Beethoven composed this sonata in 1794 or 1795, before he was twenty-five. It was in 1795 that he made his first appearance at a public concert in Vienna—a concert in aid of musicians' widows, incidentally. He played a piano concerto of his own composition, a work much more traditional than the sonatas, much more like Mozart or Haydn. But its youthful high spirits are unmistakable, as in the main theme of the last movement:

Ex. 4. Piano concerto in B flat

Soon after he had written this concerto Beethoven left Vienna on a tour of some of the main musical centres of Europe, including Prague, Leipzig and Berlin; and a few months later he undertook another, to Pressburg and Budapest. Probably he took the concerto with him and played it at some of his concerts. The tour was very successful; Beethoven wrote to his brother Johann (who had lately settled in Vienna, as a chemist): 'My art is winning me friends and fame, and what more could I ask?'

One of the greatest friends won by his art was Prince Lichnowsky, who had travelled with him on part of his journey. (Lichnowsky, a keen musician, had been a pupil of Mozart—he had travelled with him, too, on a similar tour a few years earlier.) For some time in 1794–6 Beethoven stayed in

The Young Virtuoso

Lichnowsky's house, as his guest, in return for which Beethoven dedicated several of his compositions to him. These include the first works which he thought worth an opus number (a set of three trios for piano, violin and cello) and one of the finest of his early piano sonatas, the *Pathétique*. It is one of the best known, too, and a very striking work, with its first movement full of passion and drama, and its second starting with a melody among Beethoven's most inspired:

Ex. 5. *Pathétique* sonata

But in some ways the sonata immediately before the *Pathétique* is even more striking. Its first and last movements show something of the way in which Beethoven could build whole movements out of little 'motives', or phrases consisting of just a few notes. But its slow movement is an astonishing piece. Beethoven himself said: 'It expresses a sad state of mind, portraying every shade of melancholy.' Nobody looking at the beginning of it could doubt that it is sad, tragic music (see Ex. 6 on next page): the slow, weary melody, the dark tones of the registers used, the discordant harmonies all make this quite clear. So too does the pathetic melody which follows, and the passionate chromatic music later on (and still more desolate, unhappy music comes in the continuation, not shown in our quotation).

This sonata, Op. 10 No. 3, was finished some time in the summer of 1798. It's not surprising, perhaps, that it is sombre music. Up to this time Beethoven's life had been a story of triumphs over immense difficulties, of successes achieved by the force of his genius and sheer hard work; he had attained a considerable position as a virtuoso pianist and it must have seemed that he could be certain of many, and greater, triumphs. But in 1798 he had the first suspicions of that most dreaded fate for a musician: deafness.

Ex. 6. Piano sonata, Op. 10 No. 3

III

Tragedy and Triumph

It is not easy to imagine just what deafness meant to Beethoven. As a thoroughly trained and skilled musician, with a perfect 'inner ear', he could of course hear the sound of a score simply by looking at it; and he could write down, as he always had, the sounds which came into his mind (for composers do not generally work at the piano, playing their ideas as they come).

But this was only one side of his life as a musician. He was also a pianist, and a conductor too when his own works were given. Piano playing, for which he was famous above all, would soon come to an end; so would piano teaching, if he couldn't hear his pupils playing; and so would conducting, for a conductor unable to hear his orchestra is obviously useless.

Beethoven realized all this, and more too, in those dark days in 1799 and 1800 when he noticed his hearing getting steadily worse. At first he thought it was just a passing phase, connected with other ailments (it may in fact have been caused by an attack of typhus, probably in 1796 or 1797). By 1801 he knew for certain that his deafness was increasing and that it could never be cured. For a long time he tried to keep it a secret: he knew that his reputation and career would be seriously affected if gossip about his deafness circulated. So he avoided all social gatherings, for he couldn't face having to tell people who spoke to him that he was deaf. He told just two of his closest friends, Franz Wegeler and Karl Amenda. Meanwhile, he tried various treatments, some of them appallingly painful, but only made himself feel still more wretched.

If deafness came as a tragedy to Beethoven, we, looking back on events, can see that its results were far from tragic. Up to 1800, he had visualized a career as a virtuoso pianist, travelling Europe to the applause of music-lovers everywhere. 'If it were not for my deafness,' he once wrote, 'I should by now have travelled over half the world.' But deafness changed his entire outlook: now the only career open to him was that of a composer. It affected

29

his personality, too. He could no longer communicate freely, as before, with his fellow men (or with women—and he had always hoped for marriage). So he became more and more turned in on himself, unable to share his life and its problems with others, growing steadily more odd and eccentric a person, and perhaps understandably a more aggressive one too. This was a slow process, of course; in 1800 it was only just starting, and he still had several years of active concert-giving and fairly normal social life ahead of him.

One of the products of his depression over his weakening hearing was a document which is generally called the *Heiligenstadt Testament*. Beethoven sometimes spent summers in a village called Heiligenstadt (he liked to get away from the dusty city) and when he was there in the autumn of 1802 he wrote this very strange document. It is a kind of will, addressed to his two brothers: it describes his state of mind and his bitter unhappiness over his affliction, and it is written in terms which suggest that he thought death was near.

But although the *Heiligenstadt Testament* was obviously written in great distress, it shows two important points which gave hope for the future. First, he was now resigned to whatever fate was in store for him, and no longer felt unable to face the future (he had even thought at one time of suicide). Second, his desire to write music was more powerful than ever: 'It seemed to me impossible,' he wrote, 'to leave this world before I had produced all the works that I felt the urge to compose.' Not all the music he wrote at this time reflects his unhappiness—the Spring Sonata, for example, is one of his most graceful works (Ex. 7 on facing page).

But about the time of this crisis in his life, Beethoven's musical style began to change. We saw in the last chapter how his music had the brilliance and force, even the defiance, of a young man. Now, as he passed into his thirties, it gradually began to acquire new and deeper qualities, as he moved into what is usually called his 'second period' (or 'middle period'; students of his music generally reckon that his life and work fall naturally into three stages).

What do we mean when we say that a composer writes deeper music? A word like 'deeper' really describes only how we ourselves feel on listening to it—more moved or affected—and this is a personal matter, as different people react in different ways. But most of us who like Beethoven's music can feel this difference between the works of his three periods, so it's worth thinking more carefully about the changes in his music that took place at this time.

Ex. 7. Violin and piano sonata, Op. 24 (Spring)

The most obvious one is that the works he was now writing are, mostly, longer. He didn't do this simply by writing longer melodies. But this is a part of it. Here is the opening of a string quartet, composed in 1806:

Ex. 8. String quartet, Op. 59 No. 1

Fairly fast

It is very obvious from this theme that the work which is going to follow is a long one—somehow it has a sense of space. This sense of space comes not

Beethoven's ear trumpets

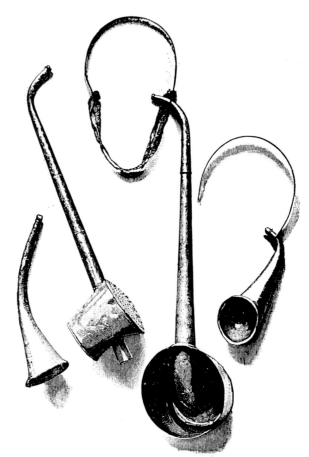

The piano presented
to Beethoven by
Thomas Broadwood

Fidelio, the final scene

Therese von Brunswick

only from the melody itself but equally from the harmony, which changes just once in the whole eighteen bars. When you examine the actual melody, you can see that it is made up of a few short phrases repeated in different ways and at different pitches. Through this method of building up all the themes of a movement out of brief ideas, even if these ideas are not themselves specially interesting as tunes, Beethoven made it possible to compose longer movements which hold together and don't just seem like a succession of different melodies. Before Beethoven, Haydn in particular had done the same sort of thing, but on a smaller scale.

One of the biggest of Beethoven's works of this period is his third symphony: it is three-quarters-of-an-hour's music (the longest symphony by Haydn or Mozart takes about twenty-five minutes). The third symphony is called the *Eroica* (meaning 'heroic'). The hero Beethoven had in mind was Napoleon. We have seen how Beethoven was a passionate believer in the rights of human beings, their freedom and their equality. Napoleon seemed to Beethoven to be a great man who stood squarely for these rights. But in 1804 Beethoven, hearing that Napoleon had proclaimed himself Emperor, realized that his hero was an ambitious man and likely to become a tyrant, as so many emperors had. He tore the title-page from his score in rage and disillusionment, throwing it on the floor; the score now says, in Beethoven's handwriting (in Italian), 'Eroica Symphony, composed to celebrate the memory of a great man.'

The symphony's heroic character is clear. Its second movement is a sombre funeral march, suitable for the burial of a military hero:

Ex. 9. *Eroica* symphony

In his first two symphonies, written in 1800 and 1802, Beethoven had written rather light movements for his finales. Here the last movement had to be on the same grand scale as the rest of the work if it were not to be an anti-climax. Beethoven made it a theme and variations, taking for the theme one which he had previously used in smaller works. The unusual feature is the way it is presented. First we hear an abrupt little theme,

Ex. 10a. *Eroica* symphony

followed by some variations on it; but this is really only the bass to the real theme, as you can see:

Ex. 10b. *Eroica* symphony

Tragedy and Triumph

But it is the symphony's long first movement which is perhaps the most individual part of it. Its first theme is short and simple, nothing more than a common-chord arpeggio. This isn't one of the movements which is built round a single theme, for there are many more—and a curious feature is that none of them is particularly beautiful, or even very interesting, as a melody. All of them, in fact, are of the same type as the first; and this is a part of Beethoven's method, for the sort of lyrical, singing melody that Mozart or Schubert used would have interfered with the almost architectural kind of design, by drawing too much attention to itself. There is in fact one theme which is lyrical, and that comes where it is least expected —immediately after the movement's main climax (which is a huge orchestral discord, repeated five times), and its effect here is to relieve the tremendous tension which has been built up.

Beethoven dedicated the *Eroica* symphony to one of the patrons who had helped him, Prince von Lobkowitz: in return for the dedication the Prince paid Beethoven handsomely, and for a year after the symphony's completion he was the only one entitled to arrange performances of it. Beethoven had other friends among the aristocratic and wealthy Viennese of his time, many of them sensitive and intelligent music-lovers who recognized his genius and felt it a privilege and duty to help him. One was Count von Waldstein, an old friend from his Bonn days, to whom he dedicated the *Waldstein* sonata; another was Count Franz von Brunswick.

It was for Count von Brunswick that the *Appassionata* sonata was composed. We saw in the earlier chapters that Beethoven was always freer and at his most adventurous when writing for his own instrument, the piano, and the *Appassionata* sonata shows well how this kind of adventurousness not only survived into his middle period but also gained in power, strength and feeling. There are few openings, by Beethoven or anyone else, which are so strong in atmosphere and so original as this. The distance of two octaves between the hands gives it a special dark colouring.

Ex. 11. *Appassionata* sonata

This theme (or actually just the first half of it) comes again after an arpeggio of semiquavers, but now it is interrupted, as though by outbursts of uncontrollable temper; it is easy enough to see why the sonata, with such violence and passion, is called the *Appassionata*. The movement's second main theme, though calmer, is also followed by more fierce, angry music, and the contrast between the quieter, more reflective moods and the passionate ones is worked out in the course of the movement. For the slow movement Beethoven used variation form, taking a theme which has little real interest in its melody but, with its sombre harmonies, has a very strong atmosphere.

Ex. 12. *Appassionata* sonata

Beethoven finished work on the *Appassionata* in 1804. During that year he was hard at work on another project, one of a kind he had never dared attempt before. To Beethoven, like most composers of his time, opera was the most challenging musical form of all: it demanded a marriage of music and drama, so that each heightened the other. But Beethoven felt that he could not attempt an opera unless he found a dramatic subject close to his own ideals; and, anyway, he had no opportunity to compose one unless, as happened in 1804, a theatre manager asked him to. He now found such a subject, and started work on an opera which he called *Leonora*.

IV

Beethoven the Dramatist

It was in 1803 that Emanuel Schikaneder, the man who had written the libretto of Mozart's *Magic Flute* (and had sung the role of Papageno in it), asked Beethoven to collaborate with him on a new opera. At that time Schikaneder organized the performances at one of Vienna's two opera houses; but soon after Beethoven had started work—the new opera was to be called *Vestas Feuer* ('The Fire of Vesta')—Schikaneder lost his position at the opera house and, with no likelihood of the opera's ever being given, Beethoven stopped work on it.

Beethoven's appetite for composing opera was now aroused. He had very definite ideas on the kind of opera he wanted to write: no lightweight love-story, like those Mozart had used in *The Marriage of Figaro* or *Così fan tutte*, would suit him; any opera Beethoven wrote had, he felt, to embody his deepest feelings. Only a subject really close to his heart could draw from him music of this kind. So when, in 1804, he was invited to write an opera for production at the Theater an der Wien, he set about looking for a suitable libretto.

He did not have to look very far. In the previous dozen or so years, since the time of the French Revolution, a good many operas had been composed in France which appealed to the audience's love of freedom and hatred of tyranny. A lot of them were 'rescue operas', having as their climax (like a Western, or a television spy story) the last-minute rescue of the hero or heroine from death.

A literary friend of Beethoven's, Joseph von Sonnleithner, suggested to him a French story by J. N. Bouilly, based on an actual incident which Bouilly had been connected with; the story had already been used before for operas—once by Cherubini, whom Beethoven much admired, and by Paër —but that was no reason why Beethoven should not use it. Sonnleithner adapted the story and made from it an opera libretto, in German.

(It is worth mentioning here that there were two main kinds of opera

38

given in Vienna during Beethoven's time: Italian opera, with most of the action and discussion between characters carried out in the conversational musical style called recitative; and German opera, in which there was spoken dialogue. Both, of course, had arias, duets and numbers of that kind. Beethoven chose to write in German, the language spoken by the people of Vienna.)

Beethoven, for whom composition was always a painful struggle—his manuscripts and sketchbooks show how he made countless small changes to almost every phrase before he was satisfied—found operatic composition particularly difficult. He had little natural feeling for the theatre, and his musical upbringing, as well as his own instincts, led him to think more easily in terms of instruments than of voices. From the start he made mistakes in the composition of the opera (*Leonora*, as it was called at first, or *Fidelio*, as it became). The first overture he wrote, now known as *Leonora No. 1*, he rejected; the second (*Leonora No. 2*) he used at the opera's first performance—but it proved unsuited to the work, for although a splendid piece of music it expresses too much of the opera's actual content to be a satisfactory introduction to it.

After the first, unsuccessful performances of the opera in 1805—with many of Napoleon's conquering troops in the audience, incidentally—Beethoven was persuaded by Prince Lichnowsky and other music-lovers who had faith in him to revise the opera. He did so, with his old friend Stephan von Breuning making changes in the libretto, and the revised version was given in 1806. Beethoven realized that the overture was not ideal and altered it, though without radical changes, into *Leonora No. 3*—a superior piece of music in itself but still a long way from the right solution. It was not until 1814, when the opera, having failed again in 1806, was revised a second time (with still more changes in the libretto), that he managed to produce a really satisfactory overture, the one we now know as *Fidelio*. But we should be grateful for his mistakes for their enrichment of the concert-hall repertory. A friend of Beethoven's said that none of his works caused him as much trouble as *Fidelio*, and Beethoven himself once called it the 'crown of my martyrdom'. Only after the third revision was *Fidelio* anything of a success; and since then it has been successful in every opera house in the world.

Fidelio is a story of political oppression. It is set in a grim fortress-like prison, where the freedom-loving Florestan has been imprisoned in a dungeon for two years by the governor of the district, Pizarro. Florestan's wife, Leonora, disguised as a young man ('Fidelio'), has become an assistant jailer at the prison in hopes of rescuing him. Eventually she succeeds in doing so, in a dramatic scene in the dungeon where, with drawn pistol, she steps between Pizarro and Florestan just as the fatal blow is to be struck—and the minister of state arrives at this very moment, in time to set things right. The story gave Beethoven splendid opportunities to write music expressing emotions which meant a great deal to him: love in its highest form, justice, and humanity.

One of the complications in the plot is caused by Marcellina, the jailer's daughter, falling in love with 'Fidelio'; and the jailer gives his consent to their marriage. The perplexed Leonora has to keep up the pretence of being a man. There is a quartet at this point, where four characters in turn express their feelings. This is one of the moments when opera departs from reality—ordinary people don't usually sing together about their feelings— but at the same time it brings the situation home to the audience in a way that even the straight theatre cannot. It is as if time has stood still for a moment while we look into the characters' minds. This particular quartet is unusual in that all the singers express their feelings to the same music— entering in turn, as in a round.

Ex. 13. *Fidelio*

Quite slow

MARCELLINA

That I to him am dear Has now be-come quite plain, He loves me, that is clear;——— My hopes are not, are not in vain.

LEONORA

How That I to him am dear Has now be -

dread-ful is my fear My hopes be-gin to

The most moving moment of all in the opera comes when Leonora has persuaded the jailer to allow the prisoners (whom we assume to be innocent victims of Pizarro) to have a moment out of their cells. They stumble out into the daylight, singing of their joy at having even a few minutes' freedom:

Ex. 14. *Fidelio*

Fairly slow

The opera's climax is the moment where Leonora throws herself between Pizarro and Florestan. The arrival of the minister of state is heralded by a trumpet call; here is the passage, made all the more dramatic by an unexpected change of key:

Ex. 15. *Fidelio*

Beethoven never attempted another opera. Several times he thought of doing so—Faust, Macbeth, and Romulus and Remus were among the subjects he considered—but *Fidelio* remained the only one. The rest of his stage music consists of some overtures and incidental music for plays (including the famous *Egmont*), and two ballets. Although *Fidelio* is unquestionably one of the greatest operas of all, there is no doubt that opera was the form which Beethoven found most difficult of all to use.

One thing about Beethoven of which *Fidelio* tells us a great deal is his attitude to marriage. Beethoven himself never married, but he certainly wanted to. Nobody knows, and probably nobody will ever know, much about his actual loves. He certainly was in love several times. He had many gifted, intelligent and beautiful pupils and it was natural that he should have fallen in love with some of them. But nearly all were of noble family, and this meant that they could never marry a middle-class person like Beethoven who had to work for his living and who could not mix on equal terms with their families and friends.

Among his earliest loves was a countess, Giulietta Guicciardi—this was about 1800, when she was only sixteen. She married a count in 1803. But her cousins, Therese and Josephine von Brunswick, sisters of the Count mentioned on p. 35, are two of the most important women in Beethoven's life. They went to Beethoven for piano lessons in 1799; the same year, Josephine was married (also to a count), but was widowed after five years. In 1804 she resumed her lessons with Beethoven, and it is very clear from some letters which Beethoven wrote to her the next year that he was deeply in love. We can never know how or why their friendship ended. Perhaps their love simply cooled in the course of time. Or possibly Josephine, discouraged by her family, realized that she could never marry him, or he realized that marriage with him would demean her in the eyes of her friends and family. Or they may both have realized that Beethoven's boorish habits and ill temper, and his poor health, would make marriage impossible. And in fact there is no definite evidence that she loved Beethoven as much as we know he loved her.

It is possible that in about 1807 Beethoven was in love with Josephine's sister Therese. And there are vague records of various other attachments in the next few years. One, at least, affected Beethoven deeply: he wrote a famous letter to a woman in 1812, 'To the eternally beloved', but it may never have been sent. We know, from *Fidelio* and remarks in his letters, that Beethoven viewed marriage as 'the union of souls', and it may be that there was no woman whose soul he felt could unite with his own. Could any mortal woman conform to his lofty ideals? And, anyway, was he the sort of man who could take part in any stable relationship with other human beings, when he was so utterly devoted to his art?

V

The Mature Artist

The six years following the first performances of *Fidelio* are the ones in which Beethoven wrote nearly all of his most famous music. Between 1806 and 1812 he composed his violin concerto and his fourth and fifth piano concertos, and his fourth to eighth symphonies, as well as a Mass, many songs and a great deal of chamber music. They were, in a sense, happy years—naturally enough, for anyone would be happy creating such a succession of masterpieces. He was becoming reconciled to his deafness, which was still worsening but was not yet total.

Not all the music of these years was on a large scale. Beethoven was content to write smaller pieces, too; many of his songs were written about this time, and so were two unusually short piano sonatas. One was dedicated to Therese von Brunswick; the other, Op. 79, is among Beethoven's most simple and light-hearted music, as is shown by part of the first movement and the slow movement. (Ex. 16, on pp. 68–71.)

By this time Beethoven had to give up playing in concerts regularly. He last played a concerto in public in 1808. After that he sometimes appeared as a conductor, often for charity concerts—some in aid of those wounded in battles during the Napoleonic wars, once to relieve people made homeless by a fire, once for a hospital. Since about 1800 his works had often been given in Vienna. But when he had major new orchestral works to perform he generally organized the concert himself, partly because he wanted to be in charge of the performances, partly because he wanted to take the very considerable profits. Such concerts were few, and must have been exciting events. In his earlier days he had included music by Mozart, Haydn and others; the later ones were all-Beethoven programmes. One, in 1808 (the last at which he played a concerto, mentioned above), was advertised as follows:

44

First Part

1. A Symphony, entitled 'Recollections of Country Life', in F major [No. 6]
2. Aria
3. Hymn with Latin text, composed in the church style. . . .
4. Piano Concerto played by himself [No. 4]

Second Part

1. Grand Symphony in C minor [No. 5]
2. 'Sanctus', with Latin text composed in the church style. . . .
3. Fantasia for piano solo [improvised]
4. Fantasia for the piano which ends with the gradual entrance of the entire orchestra and the introduction of the chorus as a finale

(Nos. 3 in Part 1 and 2 in Part 2 are from the Mass which he had recently composed; the last item is the Choral Fantasia, Op. 80, very rarely played nowadays.)

Another major artistic event was in 1814, when the seventh and eighth symphonies were given. But with the end of all hopes of an active concert and teaching career long before that, he had no secure means of earning a living. So when, in 1808, he was invited to go to Kassel as musical director at the court of the King of Westphalia (Jerome Bonaparte), with a secure and generous salary, he was tempted to go—although the musical life in that fairly small city would have been very uninteresting for Beethoven, especially after Vienna. His Viennese friends and admirers naturally did not want to see the leading composer of the day leave their city. So a group of three noblemen banded together and guaranteed him a good income if he promised to remain. He did, and everyone was content—for a while. Unfortunately, the plan did not work out as well as was hoped, for one of the group died in 1812, and another went bankrupt during the troubled times of the Napoleonic wars. Beethoven, it must be said, had some strange ideas about money, and was not in the ordinary sense strictly honest. More than once he offered the sole rights in a piece of music to two different publishers or performing organizations. Sometimes he accepted an advance payment for a work, and then never composed it. We can afford to be tolerant of such behaviour in Beethoven's case. Probably it didn't seem dis-

Figure 4. Drawing of Beethoven by Lyser

honest to him, for as far as he was concerned the only kind of honesty which really mattered was honesty to his art—setting down on paper the music that was in him.

Not surprisingly, this attitude to life made Beethoven a difficult person for others to get on with. Deafness made him still more difficult. The explosive quality that so much of his music possesses was a part of the man himself. All his friends had to understand, and forgive, his suspicious character and his bad temper. Often he quarrelled with even the kindest and most understanding of them—but usually he realized after a time how badly he had behaved.

Some of his friends, as we have seen, were middle-class people like himself. Others were wealthy and distinguished members of the nobility, like the Archduke Rudolph, son of the emperor and one of the three who made regular payments to Beethoven. Beethoven dedicated several important compositions to the Archduke, who was a pupil of his for many years, among them the fourth and fifth piano concertos and a piano trio (nowadays called the *Archduke* trio). Another of the three was Prince von Lobkowitz; he and the Russian ambassador in Vienna, Count Rasoumovsky (who had commissioned the quartet we looked at on p. 32), shared the dedication of the fifth and sixth symphonies. These dedications were expressions of respect from Beethoven, and they were also intended as Beethoven's thanks for these men's gifts and money—and what finer thanks could they have wanted than to be remembered whenever Beethoven's music is remembered?

Not every dedication was in response to patronage. The violin concerto, composed in 1806, was dedicated to Beethoven's devoted friend Stephan von Breuning—the two had been friends since their childhood in Bonn, and for a time had shared lodgings in Vienna. Von Breuning's affection and loyalty had survived some pretty unkind behaviour from Beethoven; twice there were rifts between them, the later of which lasted several years. The concerto, Beethoven's only one for violin, is a gentler work than most of those for piano, mainly because the violin is so much more a 'singing' instrument than the piano. This lyrical quality is contrasted at the start with a slightly sinister, four-note drumbeat (Ex. 17, at the top of the next page). Halfway through that come four notes on the violins, slightly sinister in a way too, not because of their tone quality (as on the drums) but because the D sharp is a foreign note. This figure of four repeated notes recurs many times during the movement—sometimes on the violins, sometimes on the horns, bassoons, or very quiet trumpets, sometimes on the entire orchestra—and it sets off the smooth themes to perfection.

Ex. 17. Violin concerto

An even more famous use of contrast, of a much stronger sort, comes in the fourth piano concerto. The slow movement (the second of the three) is a dialogue between the piano and the orchestra—an idea which might seem a little obvious but was actually rarely tried by composers (for some very good reasons). This movement can remind the listener of the mythological story of Orpheus taming the wild beasts with his lute. The orchestra starts off fiercely, in octaves, to which the piano replies quietly and gently, as if pleading. Gradually the orchestra's ferocity disappears, as the piano's pleas become more and more passionate. The movement ends in utter calm. Here is the beginning, where the contrast is at its strongest.

48

Beethoven at forty-eight

Pastoral symphony: part of the conclusion of the second movement

Piano sonata in C minor, op. III: first movement

Ex. 18. Piano concerto No. 4

Being a man of a restless, unsettled kind, Beethoven had no settled home life—no wife, of course, and no one to care for him but some servants. Whether it was due to his perpetual quarrels or simply his inability to settle down anywhere, he had no permanent home in Vienna. Every few months he moved from one apartment to another. In the spring and summer he generally left the city to stay in the countryside, at some nearby spa or small country town. Often he was invited by a nobleman, with a mansion or palace away from Vienna, to stay—once, for example, he went to Eisenstadt, to the Esterhazy family castle where for many years Haydn had been the musical director.

Certainly Beethoven loved the countryside. Nowadays, when most people live crowded together in towns, we take for granted a love of natural beauty; in those times it was fairly new. The age of 'landscape gardening', when it was generally felt that the wildness of nature could be improved by man's art, was just passing. People were only now beginning to realize the value and beauty of the peace and naturalness of the countryside.

Beethoven has left us his own testimony to his love of nature. This is the *Pastoral* symphony (No. 6). Many of his symphonies fall into contrasting pairs. There is the long, mighty *Eroica* (No. 3) immediately followed by the far gentler, lighter fourth. There is the dramatic No. 5—the most popular of them all—with its famous motive

Ex. 19. Symphony No. 5

said to represent 'Fate knocking at the door', immediately followed by the *Pastoral*. And there is a similar contrast between Nos. 7 and 8.

The *Pastoral* symphony, Beethoven said, is 'not so much painting as an expression of feelings.' That is a very important remark. He said it because he did not want us to listen to the symphony as if it were an actual picture in music of places, events, or people. It is, in fact, music *about* places, events, and people, but it does not *depict* them—it is a musical reaction to them, an expression of Beethoven's own feelings about them. Even so, there is a lot in the music which is picturesque. Beethoven gave the five movements headings, as follows:

   I. Awakening of happy feelings on arriving in the country
  II. By the brookside
 III. The peasants' merrymaking
 IV. Thunderstorm
  V. Shepherds' song of thanksgiving after the storm.

Beethoven evokes the simplicity of the country with themes and harmonies far more straightforward than his usual ones, and almost suggests shepherds' pipes in the simple solos for wind instruments. The slow movement, with its gently flowing accompaniment and its many trills, suggests the calm one might feel by a brookside. At the end three wind instruments—the flute, oboe and clarinet—give actual imitations of three birds, the nightingale, quail and cuckoo; although this really does come nearer to painting than to 'expression of feeling', the passage makes a suitable and imaginative coda (or tailpiece) to a movement in a perfectly normal and regular musical form.

Beethoven's usual third movement in a symphony is a scherzo—like the minuet used by Mozart and Haydn but faster. In the *Pastoral* symphony the third movement is a dance, and naturally of a simple, rustic kind. Its middle part even suggests country dances to a bagpipe accompaniment.

Ex. 20. *Pastoral* symphony

The scherzo ends abruptly, with the storm movement interrupting it. Here again Beethoven comes near to producing from the orchestra actual sounds to represent a storm—there are thundering rolls on the drums and tremolos on the bass instruments, raindrop-like violin notes, and violent, abrupt flourishes which seem like lightning flashes. And string tremolos, together with unexpected key changes, produce a tense atmosphere. Here is how the storm ends, with the beginning of the shepherds' thanksgiving—the clarinet and horn suggest the shepherds' pipes, before the violins give out the movement's main theme (Ex. 21 on next page).

Ex. 21. *Pastoral* symphony

VI

The Silent Years

Beethoven's 'middle period', as it is usually called, came to a splendid climax in 1812 with the composition of the seventh and eighth symphonies. The Napoleonic wars had affected him in the previous few years: in 1809, when the French armies advanced on Vienna, Beethoven had covered his head with pillows to protect his ears, and when the armies left Vienna all kinds of troubles over money and food were left in their wake. In 1810 he had composed some music to a play called *Egmont* by Goethe, the greatest poet then living, and as important a figure in German literature as Shakespeare is in English. Goethe had invited Beethoven to visit him; Beethoven didn't accept, but two years later they met. Beethoven commented on the meeting only briefly, in a letter to his publisher; Goethe, writing to a friend, said of Beethoven:

'His talent astonished me; but unfortunately he has an absolutely uncontrolled personality. He finds the world detestable, and perhaps he is right —but by doing so he doesn't make it pleasanter, for himself or others. But one must pity and forgive him, for his deafness is becoming worse. . . .'

We can learn more about the effects of his growing deafness from something written by Ludwig Spohr, a prominent composer and excellent violinist of the time. Beethoven had given up normal professional concert life by now, but at a charity concert in 1814—in aid of those wounded at the battle of Hanau—Spohr heard him and wrote:

'It was no treat. First, the piano was out of tune, but that didn't worry Beethoven as he couldn't hear it. Second, there was practically nothing left of Beethoven's great virtuosity—in loud passages he banged so hard that the strings jangled, and in quiet ones he played so softly that many notes simply failed to sound.'

53

The Silent Years

After the great works of 1805–12, Beethoven entered on a period which has been called his 'silent years'. They were silent, or nearly silent, in two senses: for Beethoven himself, gradually losing the last remnants of his hearing; and in that he composed very little between 1813 and 1819. No symphonies, no concertos, practically no chamber music: all he wrote was three piano sonatas (one of them the longest and most dynamic of all, the *Hammerklavier*), two cello sonatas, some songs and some minor orchestral pieces.

Why did a composer at the height of his powers suddenly become almost silent? We can never know the answer, but we can be sure that the reasons were both external (to do with events outside himself) and internal (to do with his own difficulty in composing).

His deafness of course had a lot to do with it. As he found himself able to hear less and less, he became more and more morose, suspicious and aggressive; in a silent world, he was mostly alone with his own thoughts. In his last years he had to carry on all his conversations in writing—some of these conversation books have been preserved—and this must have made serious discussions of any personal kind almost impossible. Every artist needs the stimulus of the outside world, and its absence surely handicapped Beethoven. But Beethoven did not make it easy for his friends. So unworldly a man was he, so incapable of looking after himself properly (and too ill-tempered to keep good servants), that he perpetually lived in squalor: his clothes were ragged and dirty, his rooms frightfully littered—with music manuscripts among a mass of other things. In washing himself he used generous quantities of cold water; he found washing stimulated him while composing, and often strode across the room to note down an idea, slopping water all over the floor in the process. A few friends sometimes came to tidy his rooms and wash his clothes.

Yet there was a certain amount of routine to his existence. A friend who was with him much in his last ten years described Beethoven's usual daily procedure. On an ordinary day, when there were no special arrangements, he rose around dawn and went to his desk where, apart from one or two breaks in the morning to go out of doors (thinking about his work as he walked), he remained until his dinner time, which was two or three in the afternoon. Then he would generally go for a longer walk. In the late afternoon he would go to a favourite tavern where he would read the newspapers, unless he had earlier done so in a coffee-house—though when the British Parliament was in session he had a newspaper at home and read the debates (he was always a great admirer of the British parliamentary system). At twilight he would often go to the piano and improvise, or play on the violin or viola he kept at hand; but he couldn't really hear what he was doing and the results were agonizing to anyone else present. The winter evenings he spent at home, reading serious literature—working at his music was too great a strain on his eyes—and by ten o'clock he was in bed.

The great worry of his years from 1815 onwards was his nephew Karl. In that year his brother Caspar had died, leaving his wife Johanna and Beethoven joint guardians of the nine-year-old boy. Beethoven hated Johanna and thought she would be a bad influence on Karl, so he at once went to law to have himself appointed sole guardian. After lengthy and bitter disputes, he succeeded. But Beethoven, scarcely able to look after himself, was no fit person to look after a child as well. Although he was deeply attached to the boy, it's no wonder that Karl grew up an unhappy and wild young man, and that he never felt much gratitude or affection towards his uncle.

Still, it is the music rather than the man which really matters. All over Austria and Germany Beethoven was recognized as unquestionably the greatest composer of his day; musicians (including Weber, Rossini, Schubert and Liszt) and others felt it a privilege to be received by him. Outside those countries, it was in England that his music was most of all admired. England was a wealthy country and musically appreciative, so Beethoven was keen to go there and give concerts. Several times he made plans to do so. The first time was in 1812, when, with J. N. Mälzel—the man who invented the metronome—he thought of going to London to give performances of a feeble and noisy *Battle* symphony he had written, at Mälzel's suggestion, in celebration of Wellington's victory over the French at Vittoria. (The work includes imitations of battle noises, and various national anthems, including *God Save the King*.) The Philharmonic Society (now the Royal Philharmonic Society) gave items by Beethoven in every concert of its first season, in 1813; a few years later they commissioned three new overtures from him—but were disappointed to discover, when they came, that he had sent two old ones and one rather poor piece. The Society tried again, this time inviting him to conduct some concerts and to compose two new symphonies. He accepted, but in fact he did not go and did not write the symphonies. The Society went on trying, and invited him to London again in 1825; eventually they bought from Beethoven rights in the ninth symphony, though in the end it was performed in Vienna before Londoners heard it.

But it may well have been because the Philharmonic Society asked him to write two symphonies that he composed No. 9 at all. True, sketches for a symphony had been made some years before, but without the request he might never have got down to the actual task of composition. Composition

Figure 5. Jottings in a Beethoven sketch-book

was indeed a task for Beethoven. Some of his sketch-books have come down to us, and we can see in them how gradually, and how painfully, he built his themes, usually from tiny, uninteresting little scraps, or transformed dull, conventional ideas into imaginative, poetic ones. Always it was done by sheer hard work, by adjusting a note here and a rhythm there, then re-adjusting time and again until eventually the ugly duckling had become a beautiful swan.

But it isn't really quite the point to talk of themes. We saw on p. 33 how Beethoven used little musical figures, or motives, to construct his themes, and to construct whole movements; and by this time of his life he was using motives in a more elaborate way still. This is certainly true of the two major works whose composition occupied most of his working time from about 1818 to 1823—the ninth symphony (known as the 'Choral' since its last movement has a chorus) and the Mass in D (written for the ceremony at which Beethoven's old friend, Archduke Rudolph, was to become arch-bishop of Olomouc—though not finished until long after).

The ninth symphony, taking more than an hour in performance, is easily Beethoven's longest. There is a rugged, grand first movement, followed by the scherzo (as second movement instead of third); and then comes a very deeply felt and beautiful slow movement. Last comes the choral move-ment. Beethoven was not the first to write a choral symphony—some minor composers of his time had also done so—and at first he had planned an instrumental finale (on a theme he later used in a quartet). But it seems that he decided to state specifically here some of the ideas about Man, freedom and brotherhood which had always lain behind his music. The words Beethoven used for this movement are taken from an 'Ode to Joy' by Schiller, the most famous German poet just before Goethe. The ode had been published as long before as 1785, and had originally been intended as an 'Ode to Freedom'; for political reasons the word 'Freedom' (German, *Freiheit*) had been changed to 'Joy' (*Freude*). Beethoven had long admired it. As early as 1793 he had thought of setting it to music; he had even made occasional sketches for melodies in years between then and 1822, when he worked out the one he finally used. Schiller's Ode—or that part of it, about one-third, which Beethoven used—embodied many of the feelings Beethoven had about Man and universal brotherhood.

But before the voices enter there is an orchestral introduction. This introduction gives reminders of the three movements we have just heard, with solo music for the cellos and double-basses in between. Then comes what is often called the Joy Theme:

Ex. 22. *Choral* symphony

Moderately fast

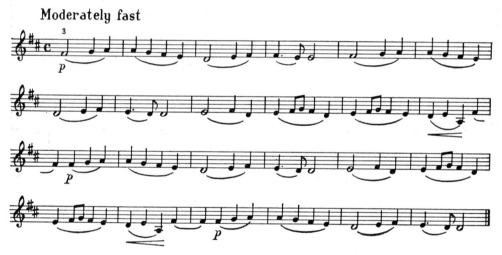

That noble melody is first given out by cellos and double-basses alone, then twice more on strings (each more elaborate than the last) and finally for full orchestra. When that finishes, the loud chord is heard again, and this time a baritone sings music like that which the cellos and double-basses had before. He sings words by Beethoven (in German):

> 'O friends, not such sounds as these,
> Instead let us strike up more pleasing ones, full of joy!'

The Silent Years

After this the baritone sings the Joy Theme, and it is taken up by the chorus.

The movement takes the form of a theme with free variations: the Joy Theme appears in different disguises to parallel the different moods of the words. Here are a few of them.

First, when the tenor sings of mankind's marching to victory (the victory of joy or freedom over sorrow or tyranny), it becomes a military march.

Ex. 23. *Choral* symphony

At a lively march speed

A different theme is stated about the middle of the movement, in the slower section which is the spiritual climax of the work.

Ex. 24. *Choral* symphony

Slow, majestic

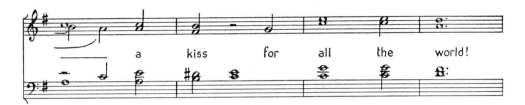

a kiss for all the world!

The triumphant choral section which follows combines this theme with the Joy Theme—rather like the process we saw in the *Eroica* symphony on p. 34, except that here it is made into a huge double fugue for chorus.

Ex. 25. *Choral* symphony

Fast

Joy, thou love-ly God be-got-ten, Smi-ling hea-ven's child di-vine,—
O ___ you mil - lions, I em - brace you!

Drunk with love, all else for-got-ten, Come we to your sa-cred shrine
Here's a kiss for all the world!

This long movement is one of the most strenuous and difficult to sing, of any music, for the chorus especially. And the sense of strain, and the huge effort which the work demands from all its performers, help to convey to listeners the mightiness of the music and of the message Beethoven tried to embody in it.

VII

'Speaking to his God'

The *Choral* symphony was finished at the end of 1823 or in the early days of 1824. Beethoven had made no arrangements for a performance, though there was talk of one in Berlin and also the possibility that the Philharmonic Society of London would perform it. But news got around in Vienna that the symphony was ready, and naturally the musicians and musical connoisseurs of Beethoven's home city wanted it to be performed there first of all.

So a group of them wrote him an 'open letter', published in the newspapers. The letter said that the Viennese were proud that he lived in their city, just as Haydn and Mozart had; that the success of Italian opera was damaging the prestige of German music; that they therefore begged Beethoven to present a performance of the symphony and show the world unmistakably who was the greatest composer.

As a result, arrangements were set in train for a performance in May 1824. An overture, part of the Mass in D, and the *Choral* symphony were given. Beethoven, of course, did not conduct. He was now completely deaf—two years before he had had the pathetic, embarrassing experience of having to give up an attempt to conduct *Fidelio*. A story is told of how he sat in utter absorption, staring at the players, and was unaware until a friend tugged at his sleeve that the audience was applauding him with wild enthusiasm.

The triumphant occasion was somewhat marred, afterwards, for several of those concerned in it. Beethoven gave a dinner party in a restaurant for the conductor, the leader of the orchestra (Schuppanzigh—a violinist he had known for many years, and a famous interpreter of his music), and Anton Schindler: during it he complained that he had been cheated of money due to him from the performance, as good as accusing them of dishonesty, and eventually they walked out, leaving him to finish the meal alone with his nephew.

A word about Schindler is needed here. He was close to Beethoven during these last years: they quarrelled several times, and once there was a long breach, but Schindler was anxious to go down in history as the composer's friend and was generally prepared to put up with Beethoven's frequent insults. After Beethoven's death it fell to him to write the first biography of the composer, as two others whom Beethoven would have preferred both refused. It is a pity this was so, for Schindler was sometimes inaccurate and, anxious to present Beethoven in the best possible light, suppressed a vast amount of information—he destroyed over 250 of the 400 conversation-books (some because they seemed to him too trivial to be worth keeping). Another biography was written soon after Schindler's by Wegeler with Ferdinand Ries, a friend and former pupil who came from a Bonn family.

Many of Beethoven's own letters survive, but they don't tell us much about him: many are business letters to publishers; many more are to friends, dealing mainly with matters of domestic routine and the like, though they do give us some idea of his sense of humour (he was very fond of puns). But on the whole they make dull reading. Beethoven was not exactly an illiterate man (he read a great deal—well-worn copies of translations of the classics, Shakespeare, and much German literature were on his shelves) but he lacked the gift, which Mozart, for example, possessed, of expressing himself vividly in words, and could scarcely even produce a grammatical sentence or a logical piece of writing.

Figure 6. Beethoven's seal, with the initials LVB

Still, it is the music that matters. The *Choral* symphony is only one of the products of these last years, of the time generally called his third or last period. (One can't say precisely when these different periods begin, but it's convenient to regard his middle period as starting just after the crisis over his deafness and his last period as starting just after the crises over his nephew Karl.) The chief works of these last years were, besides the *Choral* symphony and the Mass in D, a group of piano works and a group of string quartets.

The largest of the piano works is a set of 33 variations. The theme for these variations was a trivial little waltz tune circulated to many leading composers by a publisher, Diabelli, who wanted for a publishing stunt a set of variations, each by a different composer. Beethoven proudly refused, but then grew so fascinated with the tune that he wrote a complete set himself— a huge and masterly work. Variation form appealed to him particularly in these last years; somehow the idea of wresting every possible drop of meaning from a musical idea seems to fit in with his outlook at this time. Another form which he used a good deal in these works was fugue—and that's rather unexpected, as it wasn't at all a popular form in these years, being generally considered rather out-of-date. Fugue gave him opportunities for a kind of musical expression different from anything he had tried before.

Of Beethoven's last four piano sonatas, two have fugues and two have variation movements. What links them all is the strange, almost unearthly feeling in them: side by side there are violent, complicated passages and utterly serene ones. Even the actual piano sounds he asks for in these sonatas are odd. Here's an example:

Ex. 26. Piano sonata, Op. 110

The contrast between violence and serenity is typical of the last four sonatas. But somehow the music remains unified, despite it; it is a measure of Beethoven's greatness that a single work can cover such a range of feeling as these do and still make sense as music. Single quotations cannot give much idea of the nature of these sonatas: their size and difficulty are so important a part of them. The second of the two movements of the last sonata of all is an arietta ('little air') with variations. The arietta theme, although it provides material for some stormy writing in the variations, is an example of Beethoven at his most serene:

Ex. 27. Piano sonata, Op. 111

Very slow and simple, with singing tone

In 1822 a young Russian nobleman, Prince Galitzin, visited Vienna. On returning to St. Petersburg, he wrote to Beethoven asking him to write up to three new string quartets, for which he was prepared to pay any fee. Beethoven accepted. To such composers as Haydn and Mozart, chamber music for strings had been the works in which they wrote in their freest and most personal style, and at this stage of his life the idea of writing quartets was very attractive to Beethoven (he was thinking of writing one even before Galitzin's letter came). String quartets are often thought of as the purest form of all: every note really matters, and the most fine shades of expression are possible.

These quartets are sometimes regarded as very 'difficult' music. This isn't true. What is true is that one or two or three hearings disclose only a little of what is in them. They are music one can listen to again and again, and find more each time. A story is told about a rehearsal of these quartets, at which Schuppanzigh, the first violinist, complained to Beethoven that one passage was almost impossible to play. 'I can't think about your miserable violin when I am speaking to my God,' exclaimed Beethoven in reply.

One thing that makes the late quartets seem more difficult is that the usual conventions of musical form are often ignored. There are five quartets altogether—once started, Beethoven did not feel like stopping at the three Prince Galitzin had asked for—and only two of them are in the usual four movements.

Like the late sonatas, these quartets are full of strong contrasts. There are often abrupt changes of speed or of mood, made all the stronger in effect by Beethoven's use of very short motive-like themes, in most of the fast movements. Although many of the main movements are in something like sonata form, variations and fugue are both used. The slow movement of the A minor is a kind of variation movement, with two sections varied in turn. Beethoven wrote this movement in 1825, after a serious illness, and headed it 'Holy Song of Thanksgiving to God from one recovered from sickness'. Here is its first section and the beginning of the second:

Ex. 28. String quartet, Op. 132

Very slow and smoothly

Beethoven at fifty-five, from the bust by Schaller, 1826

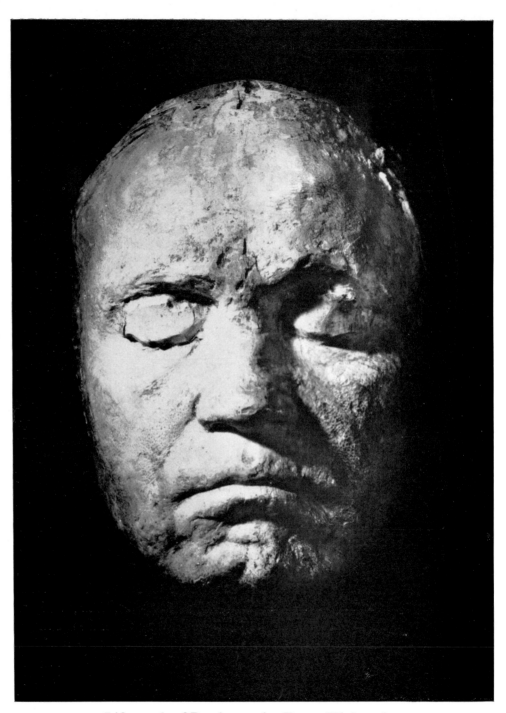

Life-mask of Beethoven by Franz Klein, 1812

faster

Lovely as this movement is, the two slow movements of the B flat are even stronger in appeal and can easily move a listener to tears. Beethoven himself said of one of them: 'No piece I have composed has moved me so deeply, and even to remember the emotions it arouses always causes me to weep.' The B flat was originally the longest of the three, with a tremendous fugue, taking some twenty minutes, as its finale. But some of Beethoven's friends persuaded him that it was too exhausting to play, and even to listen to, in this form. Eventually he wrote a new finale, but this lightweight rondo is apt to seem a trivial ending to a mighty work—better to have the original finale (now sometimes played separately as the 'Great Fugue') and put up with the exhaustion! The C sharp minor is the most mysterious of all, beginning with a fugue of unearthly stillness. Its heart is a long and very free variation movement; it also has two scherzo-like movements, and two extremely brief but emotionally intense ones as the fourth and sixth. These last quartets are by no means only slow and soulful music: there is violence and fierce tension in them as well as rapt contemplation. When Beethoven was 'speaking to his God' there was much to be said.

The five late quartets were the last music Beethoven was to write. He had further plans: he started a string quintet, and there were themes for another symphony in his sketchbooks. But he was not to live to complete them. For many years Beethoven had not been in particularly good health; he was in his mid-fifties by now, not a bad age for a man to reach in those days. During the summer of 1826 an event took place which greatly distressed him: his nephew Karl tried to commit suicide. Karl recovered, and arrangements were made for him to enter the army. In the meantime he needed to go to the country to recuperate, and it was eventually agreed that uncle and nephew would stay at the home of Beethoven's brother Johann, a day-and-a-half's journey from Vienna. Beethoven was unhappy there, not liking his sister-in-law and worrying about his nephew. In December, after a quarre lwith his brother (entirely of his own making), he rushed back to Vienna, without waiting for a proper coach; it was bitter weather and he contracted an illness, probably pneumonia.

He never fully recovered. Most of his remaining three months were spent in bed, suffering from jaundice and dropsy. He was able to read publisher's proofs of the *Choral* symphony and a string quartet, and to write some letters —including two to his old friend Wegeler, one to a London friend thanking him for some Handel scores, and one to the Philharmonic Society thanking them for a gift of £100 (which deeply touched him) and promising to send his tenth symphony.

Gerhard von Breuning, the thirteen-year-old son of Beethoven's friend Stephan, often visited him in these final weeks. He was a friendly, cheerful boy, always willing to run errands; he told afterwards how, at Beethoven's request, he passed the large Handel volumes from the piano to the bed, and Beethoven said: 'I can still learn from Handel—he is the greatest, the ablest of them all.' He also brought Beethoven books by Schiller and others, and cheered him by showing him the pictures of classical Greece and Rome in his school books.

But it was Schindler, of course, who was with him most of all in these last weeks and did the most to look after him. Once, to distract him from his suffering, he placed some songs by the young and still little-known Franz Schubert before him. 'Truly, there is a divine spark in Schubert,' Beethoven exclaimed, and he kept the songs by him several days for study. (That spark, too, was soon to be snuffed out.) Schubert was among the many Viennese musicians who visited the great man on what everybody now began to realize was his death-bed.

In spite of the best available medical care, and several minor operations, his condition steadily worsened. In March 1827, in the presence of his brother Johann and his wife, Schindler, von Breuning and another friend, he received the last sacrament of the church. Some special medicinal wines arrived on March 21; 'A pity—too late,' murmured Beethoven. On the 26th, late in the afternoon, Beethoven lay in his room, watched over by a friend, Anselm Hüttenbrenner. Hüttenbrenner tells us of the end:

> 'There was a vivid flash of lightning which illuminated the room, then a peal of thunder. Beethoven opened his eyes, raised his right hand and looked up for a few seconds, his fist clenched, with a serious, threatening expression. . . . When he allowed the raised hand to sink down, his eyes half closed. My right hand supported his head, my left was on his chest. Not another breath, not another heart-beat.'

He died as he lived, in defiance of the world.

Ex. 16. Piano sonata, Op. 79

etc.

Fairly slow

Suggestions for Further Reading

Anyone wanting to read in more detail about Beethoven's life and work would do best to start with Marion Scott's sympathetic and readable book in the Master Musicians series. The biggest and most detailed biography was written at the end of the nineteenth century by an American, Alexander Wheelock Thayer; as research has brought more and more of the facts surrounding Beethoven's life to light, it has been revised; the most recent revision, by Elliot Forbes, is the fullest account of his life now available.

The latest (fifth) edition of Grove's *Dictionary of Music and Musicians* has a useful, informative article on Beethoven by William McNaught. (The article on him in earlier editions, by Sir George Grove himself, is available in a book along with Grove's articles on Schubert and Mendelssohn.) There is a biography of Beethoven, attractively illustrated with a large number of contemporary pictures, by Erich Valentin. The very first biography, by Beethoven's friend Schindler, is available in English, with explanatory notes; and Beethoven's own letters are also published—complete in three volumes (translated and edited by Emily Anderson) or in a paperback selection of the more interesting ones (edited by Alan Tyson).

A lot has been written on the music itself. There are helpful books on the piano sonatas by Eric Blom and Edwin Fischer, and Sir Donald Tovey's prefaces in his edition are useful too (the edition itself can also be recommended). Tovey's analytical notes on the orchestral works, in his *Essays in Musical Analysis*, contain a good deal of wisdom; on the symphonies there is a book by Sir George Grove; and there is a valuable book on the string quartets by Philip Radcliffe.

Summary List of Beethoven's Works

Nine symphonies
Five piano concertos
One violin concerto
One triple concerto
Sixteen string quartets
Septet for strings and wind
Five string trios
Seven piano trios
Piano and wind quintet
Ten sonatas for piano and violin
Five sonatas for piano and cello
Thirty-two piano sonatas
Miscellaneous piano music
      (variations, bagatelles, rondos, *etc.*)
Opera, *Fidelio*
Masses in C and D
Cantatas
Songs for voice and piano
Incidental dramatic music (for *Egmont* and other plays)
Ballet, *Prometheus*
Concert overtures

Index

Index